www.tredition.de

AF178609

Andreas Bielmeier

faces

www.tredition.de

© 2021 Andreas Bielmeier

Verlag und Druck:
tredition GmbH, Halenreie 40-44, 22359 Hamburg

ISBN
Paperback: 978-3-347-23879-4
Hardcover: 978-3-347-23880-0
e-Book: 978-3-347-23881-7

Das Werk, einschließlich seiner Teile, ist urheberrechtlich ge-
schützt. Jede Verwertung ist ohne Zustimmung des Verlages
und des Autors unzulässig. Dies gilt insbesondere für die elekt-
ronische oder sonstige Vervielfältigung, Übersetzung, Verbrei-
tung und öffentliche Zugänglichmachung.

for my best friend, the crazy horse-lady

in eternal love

The world keeps on existing even if I am gone.

lonely boy

He's sitting in the church
praying to God
for a better life
for his mother and his sister.

He's dead inside
most of the times,
crying on his own
lonely nights and lonelier dreams.

It's the end of december,
he awakes,
another year older
just wants somebody to heal him.

Another one in his bed
ghostin´ in his mind
lets him sleep restless,
the fear of being left.

He's not feeling alive,
the fire burns him down,
waiting for love
until the end.

No one dares to ask
cause no one can see.
He´s invisible,
alone.

He showed me the stars
in his darkest nights.
Our clothes beside his bed,
I don't belong here.

We´re dancing to the beat
at summer days,
the pretty boy
my oh my.

Say that you miss me
cause I miss you.
Guess you kissed the others
like you did with me.

Drunk enough to realize
you
look at me
most of the time.

He closed the cage,
mid August.
I let him fly
the lonely boy.

shadow games

You hurt people
with your guilty pleasure.
Once we were friends
now I despise you.
It's almost midnight,
you are not in your own bed.
Acting innocent
the next day
but come back in the sunset.
A touch of your perfume
is always in the air.
I wonder if your boyfriend doesn't mind.
Came to earth
to bring out the worst in people.
The shadow games are funny
just for you.

before

Firestorm
in my mind.
Cursed the love,
looked for glory just for fun.

I can taste the alcohol.
You're a little to much for me,
I'm a bit to much for you.
Wishing me a world.

Running in my nightmares.
I don´t understand.
And now I´m loveless
in the great cold.

In my head
you´re still alive.
Stole my soul.
The visions never stop.

Split up my life
into after and before.
I was pure
before.

turn me as the world turns

plastic dolls

We can never be friends
or something like this.
Think you know my ex,
everyone knows you.
Sleeping in big cities,
empty beds at home.
Drink and sleep.
Bury me in silence.
Lately you've been living the dream.

All I know is
that Plastic Dolls
know the fun
of funerals.

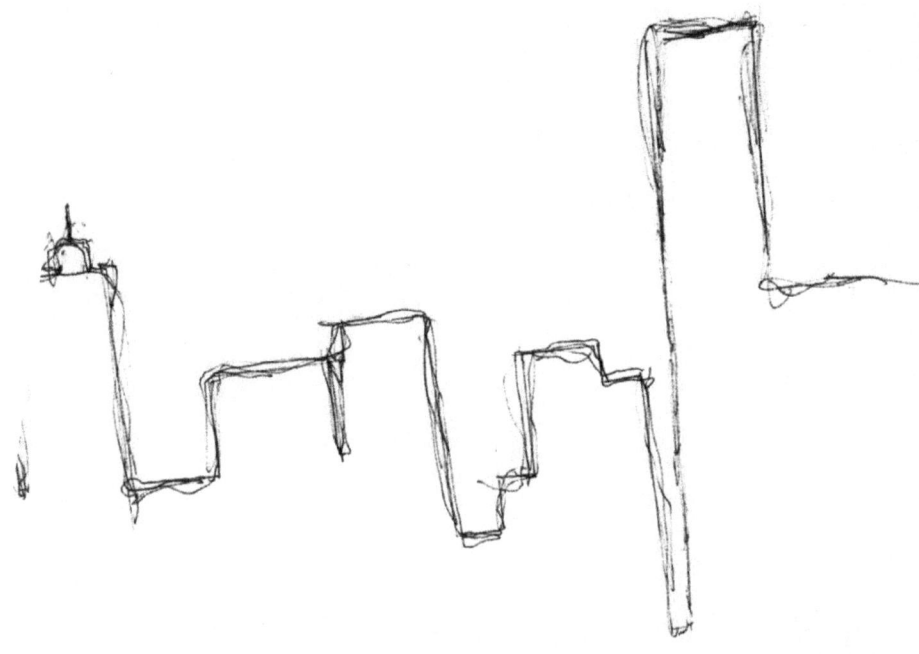

I answered the phone and hoped it was you. *Hello* I said. *Hello* you said. All was well this day.

a song for infidelity

Howling sirens in the background.
You came to my hometown
with a dirty secret.
I was obsessed to disclose.
A good thing
I don´t know you that well.
I´m hot on your heels.
Watch you leave a strangers house,
on tiptoes
with your shoes in your left hand.
What happens behind closed doors?
A good friend of you showed me the hidden place
where you clean your laundry.
Your secret is no longer a secret,
I think he knows.
You played him a song for infidelity.
He knows this song so well,
he can sing along.

madness is fun

All the tears are just a show,
all the screams are just for him
and all the fears are just for attention.

She left her hometown
to see the world and conquer the guys,
but came back alone.

Riding ponies in Puerto Rico,
a pinot grigio for breakfast,
acting drunk to play the main role.

Big stories of bigger adventures,
all made-up.
Just stories.

She's a better storyteller than I am,
think she should have written this book
and this text about herself.

hear the foxes cry

A midnight walk
full moon in the sky,
reflected stars

A little village in the woods,
Fire in the fireplace,
Quiet beats in the background

You taste like cherries in the summer,
a shame that I don't like neither cherries
nor the summer

Morning sun
kisses my face,
a step in the dew

I left footprints on the floor
you think they guide you into wonderland,
begged me for my love

I'll send you into exile

to your gold and to your diamonds

to cry down your hopes

You can't imagine the pain I had because of you.

boundaries

i tried to keep on
but i failed

pages burn and i'm burning with them
my skin is covered in ashes
my heart stopped beating
in my thoughts i'm still 18
i can feel
the water in my eyes
you still haunt my house
i shoot down the ghost of you
i am a dangerous man
but i give you 5 seconds
i really like
the boundaries around you

In the beginning *me*, in the end *me*, in between *us*.

free. for the night.

the hunter

Not a friend
not yet an enemy.
A killer,
words as weapons.
Expectations
tie him up.
Head in the hoodie,
a little love.
Lost at last.

homeland

Summer days
barefoot in the garden
barefoot in your kitchen
apples from the apple trees
chickens cackle
our little farm

Autumn evenings
glowing candles
colourful leaves
sleepovers
heavy duvet
kept me warm

Winter nights
snowflakes melting
on the windows
crackling fire
christmas eves
now you´re gone forever

Spring mornings
dew on grass
standing on your grave
knowing you were proud
birds over my head
remind me of my homeland

It's a tragedy, the things you did.

pool parties

Go with the wave they say.

Our day should be celebrated down in France.

It's 10 pm and it's getting dark,

your legs are dangling in the water.

I swim one more round.

The boys turn up the music,

we´re just kids, enjoying the summer.

I watch these scenes from the outside

like a stranger or a stalker

but the memories just feel so good.

jupiter devotee

We've met in July
the summer I turned 20.

We partied the Saturday Nights
and escaped the Sundays.

Taught me some lessons for life:

Number 1: The high was worth the trouble!
Sometimes I miss my old friends
made some new friends.
But in the end it doesn't matter.

Night has almost gone
and we're not sober anymore.

Number 2: Don't care about jealousy!
I am not as rich as Caesar was
or as famous as Picasso.
But in the end I´m not alone.

Nippin´ the last sip of wine
turn up the music.

Number 3: The Shame is all the same!
Oh when we first met
never thought this could happen.

We fell for each other. But at the wrong time.

vino girls

In the City of the Angels,
in the pale fog of the night,
somewhere howles a wolf.

Dancing with our shoes off,
the whole gang
of the Vino Girls.

And we can´t stop
and we won´t,
till we see the sunlight.

Our night, our Time,
more than a sober love.
The ribbons are getting stronger.

Days like these
I want to stop time.
A wizard showed me how.

Eve, Midnight, New Moon.

Time´s ours,

Distance´s not.

The melody stuck in my mind.

And there was this lake

we used to meet - again.

For now we´re dancing

in the rain

with our Vino girls.

hugs from a friend

sweet
your walk
your smile
and how you always treat me right.

You open a candy shop
and give away everything.

Pouring rain above my head,
the umbrella keeps me dry.
Watching the rainbow appear.

spicy
your tongue
your words
and your speeches for the underdogs.

The more you fight
the more you get.

Let's paint the world in colours,
small symbols and large drawings.
Rainbows everywhere.

loud
your voice
your mind
and your sense for justice.

The sky is full of colours,
keep on painting,
keep on loving.

liar

I call you a liar
´cause you lied to me
most of the time
about your past.
I thought
you'd be different.
I still hear the raindrops
on the water
under the bridge
on the big river
we sat
and kissed.
I still feel the food
on my tongue,
in the restaurant
of the little woman,
we ate
and laughed.

I still cannot see
because of the tears.
They hurt my cheek.
I still swear to God
not to trust again
somebody
who lied to me.

angel rest on earth

Laughin' loud
in quiet nights.
The summers in our 20's,
ice cream in the parks.

Playin' games,
getting lost
in our thoughts.
Moonlight in the lakes.

Sharin' secrets.
Learned a lesson for life.
You have the light in you.
Just turn off the darkness.

Gettin' that LA feeling
even though we've never been there.
Balcony parties with our friends
music takes us away.

Puttin´ on my sunglasses
like in an undercover mission.
Young girl with younger eyes,
an old soul and an older heart.

Dreamin´ quiet
of louder days.
Heaven´s mine.
My angel rests on earth.

I wanna feel something.

But just the good things.

That's why I don't feel anything.

so far away

Now you're in heaven
and the world became more quiet.
Childhood friends,
grew up together.
A million miles,
so far away.
I've forgotten how to cry.

is there life on mars?

He said
I wanna go
to see the world.
And I´ve told my therapist.

Your gifts look like
they were made for me.
And when you´re gone
I´ll cry a lot.

Take me with you,
on the highest mountains,
the deepest oceans.
Paradise is everywhere with you.

Dancing like in the 80s,
side to side with you.
Shiny disco balls,
footloose on the dancefloor.

A call
in the middle of the night,
said that you need me
now.

Is there life on Mars,
Like the tingle is in me?
Take you to jail
so you can rot in shame.

role model

We drank champagne under the streetlight.
One day in the past.
Breath in the cold air,
choke on your lies.
Time goes by
and my wounds hurt less.
We have dried our tears,
now I do it on my own.

disaster

You´ve dated too many guys,
heard too many lies
and now you did the same to me.

And I asked you:
How do you sleep?
You said you don´t.

And in the cold september nights
the rain felt even colder
but I was trembling with fear.

Set my mind on fire.
Ice cubes in my heart.
Everything's just black or white.

I´m bad at love
and so are you.
Obviously.

We talked but never really communicated,
we loved but never loved each other,
and then we said goodbye.

You whispered in my ear: I don't want you to get married.
And I answered: Why now? You´ve had all these years
to tell me.

thundersnow

Sometimes you don´t know
who you are
and where you belong.

Trapped in a live,
a game like hide and seek.

I know stories about you
awkward and kinky.

Like a thundersnow,
not a snowflake,
not yet a thunderstorm.

And the flash is only in your mind,
keep on moving,
it starts with accepting.

When you're home alone,
on your couch,
this´ a dangerous game.

You know some tricks
to talk to me in illicit ways.

Like I'm sitting in a train,
miles away
from now.

I was just looking
for someone like me,
but the thundersnow blinded my hopes.

body heat

Feels like
we've met before.
This feeling
I can't compare with nothing.
Stronger and a little bit bad.
And you made me feel crazy
when you touched me.
My body heat is like
50 degrees.
The past that we share
lies in ruins.
And I wont imagine
a day after tomorrow.
I feel your cold chest
and your colder skin.
My lips lost faith in warmth.

I cry on my own. Most of the time.

toxic summer

The ribbons are torn,
the pictures are burned.
I try to forget the memories.
We've spent days and nights,
only one summer.
Poisoned my wine,
nasty and evil.
Slip on my sentences,
screaming on the sidewalk.
We never danced to happy songs
and I wasn't ready for the break.
You´ve had you complicit
and call her best friend.
Now I´m glad you´re gone.

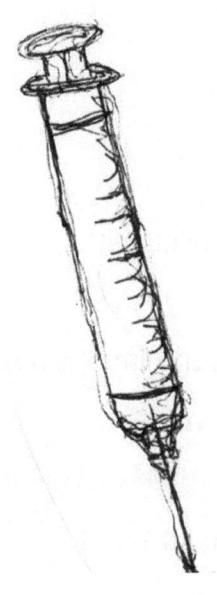

too beautiful

Oh you´re so beautiful,
just a bit too much.
With your big brown eyes
and the perfect hair,
your pure scent.

I like your face,
your pretty face,
freckles round your nose.

This new pop song in the background
for our life and our love,
feeling good as hell,
only a few days in the summer.

And while we drank
you made fun of me.
Talking shit,
every day.

Truth hurts,
hurts so much,
but not so hard,
as you hurt me.

And then I realized:
you'd never be mine,
you´re just too beautiful.

You are more beautiful than Paris in the 60's.

You burned down my house with your fires.

Your toxic fires.

The flames kissed my chest like you kissed my neck.

I begged for water, so that I can finally breathe again.

you know my songs

You know my songs,
you can sing them along.
I know your love,
but I can't empathize.
They know our story,
they dream of a similar one.

You know my ache,
and I know your weapons.
I know your hometown,
know how it looks at night.
They know nothing,
and still wanna change everything.

You knew my body,
like nobody does.
And I know your songs
but I sing them alone.

my
body
is
my
body

white aesthetics

I dreamed in black or grey,
all shadows of white.

Tigers running
through the maze.

We were young and foolish
and in love with the wrong people.

You show mercy
just for fun.

White sheets turn into dust
like glitter in the moonlight.

Roses
on the hard ground.

A coconut dream
of white beaches.

From the airplane window
city lights shine like diamonds.

After a few waves
we disappear.

United. As the tiger
and the maze.

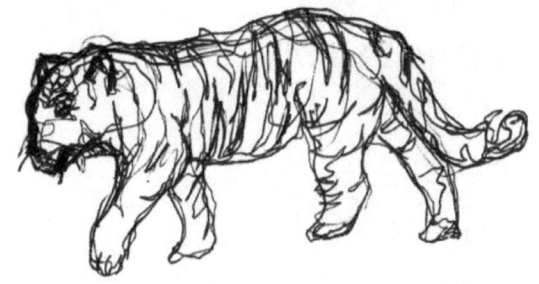

MAKE ME GOOD AGAiN

MiRROR MiRROR
WHAT'S iNSiDE.
A DEAD BOY
FiGHTiN.

DEMONS SCREAM.
SMOKE iN HiS LUNGS.
FiNDERS KEEPERS FOR HiS SENSE.

BRiGHTER FiRES.
iNTOXiCATiONS.
REFLECTiONS
OF ANOTHER LiFE.

SHADOWS
OF GREY FLAMiNGOS
iN THE EVENiNG SUN.
A FRAGMENT
OF A BETTER WORLD.

i USE
OUR VOiCE MESSAGES
AS A GOOD NiGHT STORY.
LiE TO ME
ANOTHER DAY.

NIGHTMARES
MADE ME DO THIS.
CAN'T SEE ME CRY,
I AM USED TO THIS.

EVER SINCE YOU'RE GONE
MY TABLE IS SO BIG
AND EMPTY,
MY BED FEELS LIKE CONCRETE.
YOU OWN A HOUSE,
A DOG,
THE GLITTER AND THE GLAMOUR.
I WAS YOUR BIGGEST FAN,
BECAME FAMOUS FOR BAD PROPERTIES.

i WAS SPECiAL JUST FOR THiS.
YOU SHOWED ME HEAVEN,
YOU SHOWED ME HELL.

gone in august

The baddest of them all
tried to heal me,
but also failed.

Pushed me away
to fight for a love,
without me.

I can see my baby
swimming in the ocean,
almost drowning.

To wild to stay,
to obsessed to leave the other boy,
so you left me.

Oh my God,
summer got us really hot
I missed you a lot.

I painted this picture with the blood dripping from your hands.

a puzzle piece

Thought I was complete
before.
Then I first met you.
I wasn't complete
before.

Your heart so big,
your soul so bright.
A light machine
behind your eyes.

Saw your home,
the beautiful island.

Suddenly this summer is frozen.
You can fix me
just a little.

Depression hit me really hard.
You pull me back on earth,
strengthen my roots.

You realize
that a piece of the puzzle
is missing
when you're at the end.

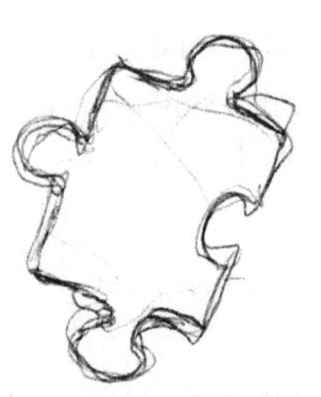

a powerful speech

Another defeat against justice,
from now on I'll count the fights.

Roses come back with thorns,
grow bigger in your bloody hands.

You quit your job and burnt down the house,
looks like you know the consequences now.

Glad it's over,
how sad it took a powerful speech.

And I don´t need your love,
it wasn´t there for years.

Please send someone
I can look up to.

I´ve been down since january
but you are still laughing.

There is no love in our hearts,
we gave it all to the good ones.

My imagination hugged me from behind,
hits me hard on the head.

It wasn't really fun to live,
but never too good to be true.

my wings

My wings helped me to fly.
I can no longer fly.
Sprayed my perfume in the air,
just to get reminded.
Creepy beats don't scare me no more.
My mind of storm
created the battlefield.
A sober night,
with stars flying around,
not just on drugs.
My wings helped me to fly,
now I fly on my own.

needy

I sit and wait for a change.
High expectations.
You won´t stay alone,
´ll find a prince and inner peace.

And if I don´t know it better
I think you´re needy by me.
Want me so bad
just for you.

crying on stage

When the curtain closes
the show is over.
And your first ex meets your last one
backstage.

You swear you changed,
but not this time.
Get angry for no reason,
celebrate the break-up-day.

Hear your bittersweet tears
drop in the cup of tea.
Have a best friend,
but how good is she really?

The whisper in the audience
screams you down.
And on your knees
you cry and cry and cry.

We all can be a part
of your performance.
Blood on your hands,
drugs in your backpack.

When the curtain closes
the show is not really over.
It continues behind the fabric
'till all of us are crying on the stage.

Dreams of our honeymoon, dreams of being loved by you.

war inside

All your jokes
are a cry for help
to get you out.
You´ve told me your story
and I listened
carefully.
There are things
I can't even talk about
with my friends.
Showed me your scars,
and I cried
the next day.
Stop touching your wound
and it will start
to heal.
Not fair,
that the world
is oh so mean.

chasing

Sometimes I ask myself
what happened to us.
The hunter and the deer
dancing in the moonlight.

Remember last night when you promised me?
Your life's the biggest lie.
Feels like I´ve grown a lot
over the past year.

Dedicated my tears to you
and became even stronger.
And I have sworn that my happiness will never
depend on another person's decisions.

I found out on Sunday and left you on Monday,
but on Wednesday you loved your next.

my first best friend

We thought it'd last forever
but it wasn't meant to be.
Meetings after school,
secretly smoked cigarettes.

We were younger
in the summer of 2012.
Shared our dreams,
you were my first bestie.

Made some new friends,
but when we met
I still remember
every afternoon together.

the beauty and the more beauty

And I get really jealous
when I see you talking with someone else.

A summer romance.

You only call me when you're drunk
and whisper sweet things to me.

I want my honeymoon.

Dance to pop music
crying to love movies.

More than a material boy.

All seemed so easy,
kisses in slow motion.

Marry me with paper rings.

Break my bones
by the ocean.

Glitter rain on me.

I´ll run to you,
please come to me.

Pillow thoughts
keep me awake.
But I blame it on the drinks.
So I´m daydreaming.

drink to forget

There was a girl with her sleeves to long
and her clothes to old.
But we were friends for many years.

Haven't seen my school friends for a while.
Is the blond one still alive?

We gossiped over the table
about Mrs. English-Teachers problems.

And when we meet again,
we drink to forget,
to never forget our time.

I was super wild.

good creature

I saw you first in January,
surrounded by golden strings,
a shining charisma.

You dropped your hand off my shoulder,
an angel like you
deserves more than thunderstorms.

With your speeches you made me speechless.
On Dinner Parties you danced like Gatsby,
your face´s a reflection in the champagne.

A gloriole over your head,
you would have made such a beautiful fiance.
But we´re grown.

And now you can´t remember me,
cursed my name,
I forget yours too.

when the lizards awake

While I´m dancing
you´re standing still,
and while I´m crying
you´re crying more.
A superhero has fallen.
Now look at
where we ended up.
Your realm was the night
and I was the king.
I´m afraid of the day
we´ll meet again,
cause I don´t know
if I´m gonna cry or laugh or something like that.
Too busy to call me back.
The angel whose wings have been stolen.
You introduced me
to the moon and the stars,
we stared into the darkness
till the lizards awake.

Nowadays I have a dream:
my plaid blanket
on the wet grass.
You, touching me,
whispering:
I´d like to kiss you now
and me answering:
go for it.

untiteled

You promised me a love
and I wanted to believe it.
Now I'm sitting on my piano,
waiting for an answer.

You made me feel like I deserved this,
and I was so stupid and wanted it.
Now I'm lying in my bed,
waiting for changes.

You hurt me again and again
and I always wanted you back.
Now I'm writing a poem about you,
waiting for you to read it.

You wrote down a list with the most important things for you.

I wasn't 1st. Or 2d. I wasn't even the last.

queen of the mean

Judging people for their fears,
the cheaters and the leaders.

The fireworks cannot impress,
stone cold heart.

You think you´re so pretty
that everybody wants you.

Hate me now,
cause I dethroned the wicked.

And on my way up to the top
you pushed me and I felt and felt and felt.

You´re not mean,
just build walls around.
But you were a queen.

the broken hearted club

This one's for them
they do no longer believe
or hope.
For the broken guys
and the busted girls.
Like her and I.

She found love.
And I found lies
under my bed.
Haven't seen you for a while,
dunno what's going on.

A change came,
like a breath of wind.
And you left the club.
Not broken anymore.

goosebumps when you touch me

Take my hands,
making plans.

Bring me home
to your house.

Falling in love,
even with your mad touches.

Your picture in my purse.

Have no answers
to the questions I don´t know yet.

I once got goosebumps when you touch me,
but not anymore.

afternoons under the tree

No clouds in the sky of July,
phone calls in the night.
We´ve spent a couple days
under the tree.

The smoke was everything but grey,
made the hot summer days even hotter.
Picnicked in the grass,
showed you a piece of my heart.

You hate me now
and I wasn't honest with you.
My heart didn´t know the way,
drove me really crazy.

And nowadays
when I come back to the tree
that once gave us shade,
I realize, it was the fault of the time.

backstreet boys on the radio

My first crush
and you were with it.
Crashed our date,
made fun of all my exes.

We laugh at our haters,
another day,
another night,
another lunch.

A car ride in the dawn,
Backstreet Boys on the radio.
I want you to dance
with a drink in your hand.

And when I die
you'll get my money
and my dog.

Life´s not hard
when we´re together.

Found Prince Charming.
Fate brought you two
together.

Ask me to stay by your side
and you know I will.
I hope you know.

to be young and in love

She lost her identity
and he was responsible.
They fell in love on a cold winter day
with her scars
and his dreams.
Made for each other.
Why don't you guys just break up? I asked.
Twinkling sparkles in her eyes,
a grey cold fog over her house.
He just calls her baby on the weekends,
he's too busy with the other chicks.
The summer road takes them home
to their hometown.
And the breaking I heard was her heart,
dropped down in a million fragments.
How to be young and in love? I asked.
He sacrificed his dreams for her love.
But she broke up
with him.

a piece...

... of shit.

cherrypicker

Teach me
how to be bad
and feel good about it.

I swear
that my heart don't beat
when I´m not with you.

Some days
can change two lives.
This day just changed mine.

After all these years
you cannot feel sorry,
for the music and the dances.

Teach me
how to break a heart
and go without a farewell.

Held you in my arms
with your head on my chest.
Fell asleep protected.

Pushed me deeper than Miami.
How can you be so cruel?
I'd be happier without your taste on my tongue.

You always picked the best,
I always got the worst.

crazy horse-lady

Not even they can stop you now.

Savage girl.

Classy roots.

Riding the bullet.

Looking sweet like cinnamon,

bitter like Gin Tonic,

stronger than a Mojito,

spicier than a chili.

You´re not here to take a part.

You take it over.

Soulmate.

You fit me better than my best coat.

Midnight drives,

carpool karaoke.

Flawless friend.

I'm sure we´ve met in a previous life.

My existence is a *best of* you.

And the others

cannot compare at all.

But in my dreams, we´re still in love.

changes

Found a new love
after the break-up.
Looks just like me.
The holy words
drip from your lips,
forming a puddle on the floor.
No longer
the superhero,
but the villain.
You burned the flannel shirt
that you wore on our first date.
To many memories.
Packing all my things
to move on
to a new lie.
I believe in Changes.
I believed in you.

the jellyfish

Once upon a time
someone was ghostin in my mind,
swimming like a jellyfish in the ocean.
Stare me down
in the rush of sugar.

Slipped through my thoughts,
did not let me sleep.
I feel like in the fairytale
of the little mermaid and her prince.

We stand on the caravel.
Wind in your hair.
Stole my voice.
Caressed my skin.
You tie tight to me
with your tentacles.

I am running.

My memories in ashes.

The dark forest,

fogged up windows in the car.

Moves like an angel

in the water.

Talks like the devil

in my dreams.

Me against the venomous jellyfish.

We danced the night away, to the sunrise, the golden daylight.

sad.
regrettable.
shy.
woeful.
sorry.
beautiful.

sunrise kisses

I just don't know why I did this. Ran away with my be-
longings, but you tied me to bed. I´ve been the prey in
your game. You tried to lure me away. But I came back.
I was a predator, but you ate me. You consumed me like
heroin.

You left me in the kitchen like a glass of wine. Only
tasted one sip. I crawled after you for no reason. The
fire filled my lungs and I screamed. Smoke escaped my
mouth. My tongue was like liquid mercury. I died of
thirst.

The first rays of the morning sun, brighter than ever.
Opened my eyes, ate breakfast in bed alone with a cand-
le on my bedside table. I stepped into the daylight and
started living.

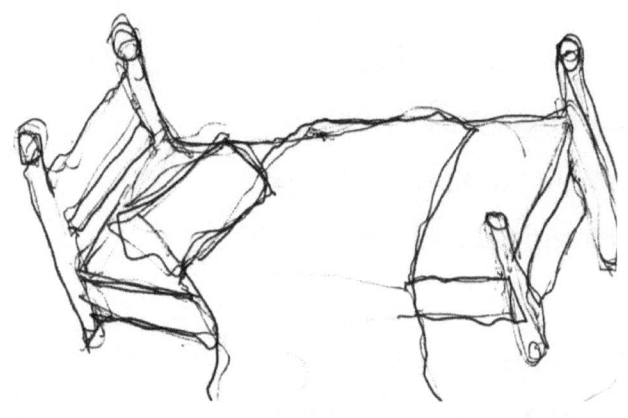

the masked ball

Money is the answer
to the question of your happiness.
The harder you fight,
the more respect you get.

But you gave up the fight,
got out of the arena as a loser.
Showed me your pretty things,
your belongings and your wealth.

The crowd just sang for you,
happy birthday and good luck.
Take off your mask,
tear down your walls.

And when you feel old
you can come back to me.
But first
burn down your gold and glory.

bad news in the morning

When I opened the newspaper in the morning
there was your name in the headline.
The big black letters told me what you did
another day with another guy.

There once was a river without water
and a love story without love.
Packed all our things for the holiday trip,
you changed the way of living just for me.

The crowd sang happy birthday,
after all the wishes and the candies.
When I was drunk I thought the stars were diamonds
and that your heart beats just for me.

Summer is over and you are still in my mind.

the curse

Try to figure out
what's going on with you.
Try to redeem you
from the curse.
Who do you call
when nobody's home?
What do you ask me
when you don't have any words.
And how do you swim in your tears?
Is it alright now?

rising star

She was standing on the rocks
with her eyes wandering over the grey sea.
Waves lashed against her ankles.

Someone said *Stars need darkness to shine*
but she needs the sunlight.

And while her voice gets louder,
and her stand gets stronger,
she becomes the sea,
and the sound of the sea is her whisper.

I wrote love letters.
For everyone I hate.
But I never sent them.

The Ghost of you is still around.

I hear your echo and feel your spirit.

I just wanted you to know that the afternoons in your garden were the best of my life.

a man, a chapter

I read you like a book
and loved you like my favorite chapter.
But you closed the book
before I finished.
Never felt something again.
My heart so shattered,
oh so many splinters.
And I was too mean
to believe in us
or in you.
Just like old movies
on the screen.
Left the perfume in your house,
just a little hint for you.
I am used to nightmares
and to the monsters under my bed.
Please don´t tell me
you never noticed me.

The elevator stopped and I said goodbye.

broken.

the prey escaped the cage.

sos - please send help.

a thousand thunderstorms over my skin.

a cliffside to jump off.

no holding hands to stop.

kisses under the streetlights are in the past.

broken bones and broken hearts.

my burning desire extinguished.

the city was so beautiful at night.

they say I'm too young to get lost.

are you gonna tell him? no.

or anyone? no.

my biggest fear and worst nightmare.

some said I did it.

I'd never go back to being broken.

A so-called-friend

Sorry for not creating you
a symphony.

new years eve

We spent time
and time passed by.
Snowflakes on the window,
watched them melting,
like I did in your arms

First you kissed me down
and then you let me go.
I cried in the car
on my way home.

And I hope that you know I'm sorry.
Year after year
on New Years Eve.

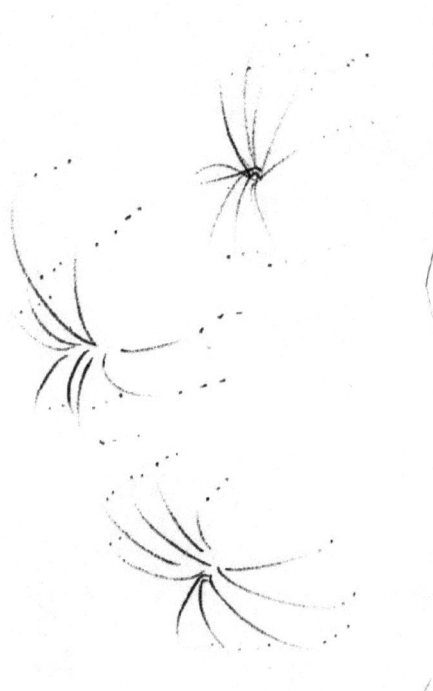

I always thought the hardest thing existing is a diamond.
But it's your heart.

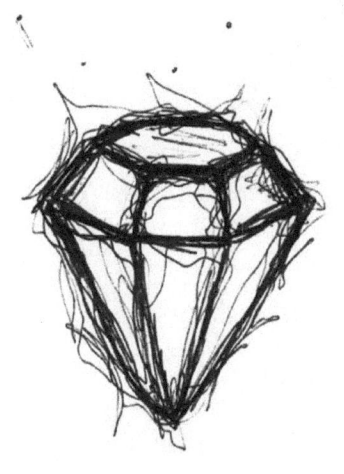

i was 1st

yeah I got your message
but I haven't read it yet
and I won´t

it's not meant to be
a secret obsession
confidential touches

think
we took something like drugs
cause I felt really high

nostalgic crying
on my way home
crescent moon, nearly 1 a.m.

stick a price thereon
I´m five dollars
but you asked for a free ride

all of my places are ruined
and now I´m alone
I'm torn

you don't belong to me
you never did
I was just the first

girl on the dancefloor

Roots on earth,
thoughts in the sky.
We get down every Saturday night,
the beat is our heartbeat.

Dancing ´til we can't no more,
the taste of Tequila.
Dust like snow
in the neon lights.

King and queen
of the prom.
Flying high
on the dancefloor.

And there´s one to make me dance
and one to make me breathe.
And one to make me live,
music keeps us alive.

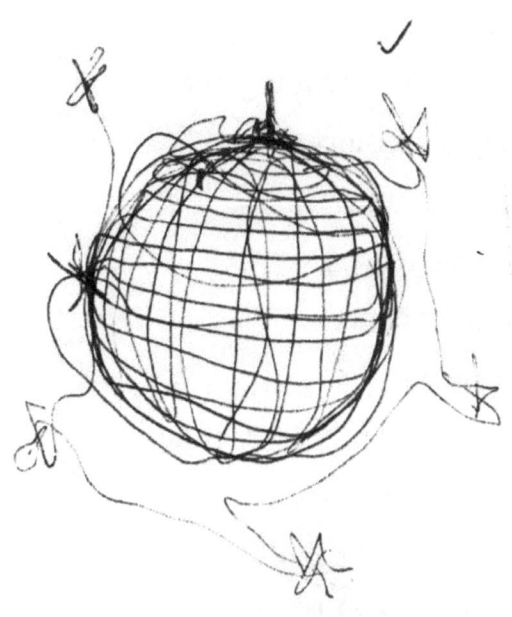

i hate you - but not a lot

Wait…
That's a lie.
I hate you a lot,
and every day we've spent together
and every single memory.
All the pain
and you were the reason.
Just hang up the phone.
Let's talk seriously.
I'm independent and much wiser now.
The reasons are shit
and it was no one else's fault.
Pushed me down the cliff
with a hidden knife.
And when my head hits the water
I scream that
I hate you - A lot.

I woke up today - happy.

bring it to an end...

Thank you Vanesa for the drawings. I love the cover, you did a great job (The jellyfish is still my favorite). Working with you is always an inspiration.

Thank you Sandra. You knew the stories before I did. And you read them first. You make me feel like I can do everything, everyday.

And thank you Nadine. I know you are my biggest fan. Hugs and kisses.

Zeitfracht Medien GmbH
Ferdinand-Jühlke-Straße 7
99095 Erfurt, Deutschland
produktsicherheit@kolibri360.de